Round the Year
Cookbook

by Sue Fisher
illustrated by Ken McKie
photographs by Tim Clark

Spring Recipes

Hot Spicy Pork
Banana Crunchy Pie

·

Quick Chilli con Carne
Apricot Bordelaise

·

Plaited Cheese Slice
Rhubarb Fool

·

Haddock Deane
Orange Tangoes

·

Easter Lamb
Hazelnut Cheesecake

·

Italian Liver
Soufflé Omelette

AUTUMN

VEGETABLES
Beetroot
Brussels Sprouts
Cabbage
Carrots
Cauliflower
Celery
Cucumber
Leeks
Marrow
Mushrooms
Onions
Parsnips
Potatoes
Spinach
Swede
Sweetcorn
Turnips
Watercress

FRUIT
Apples
Bananas
Blackberries
Damsons
Grapefruit
Grapes
Lemons
Melons
Oranges
Pears
Pineapples
Plums

FISH
Bream
Brill
Crab
Carp
Clams
Cod
Dabs
Dover Sole
Grey Mullet
Haddock
Hake
Halibut
Herring
Lemon Sole
Lobster
Mackerel
Mussels
Plaice
Prawns
Rainbow Trout
Red Mullet
Rock Salmon
Salmon
Scallops
Sea Trout
Shrimps
Skate
Sprats
Turbot
Whiting
Winkles

MEAT
Duck
Goose
Grouse
Hare
Rabbit
Scotch Beef
Scotch Lamb
Turkey
Venison
Welsh Lamb

WINTER

VEGETABLES
Beetroot
Broccoli
Brussels Sprouts
Cabbage
Carrots
Cauliflower
Celeriac
Celery
Cucumber
Leeks
Mushrooms
Onions
Parsnips
Potatoes
Spinach
Swede
Watercress

FRUIT
Apples
Bananas
Grapefruit
Grapes
Lemons
Oranges
Pears
Pineapples
Rhubarb
Tangerines

FISH
Bass
Bream
Carp
Cod
Coley
Dabs
Dover Sole
Haddock
Halibut
Hake
Herring
Lemon Sole
Mackerel
Mussels
Native Oysters
Plaice
Rainbow Trout
Salmon
Scallops
Skate
Sprats
Turbot
Whiting

MEAT
Australian Lamb
Duck
English Beef
Hare
New Zealand Lamb
Pheasant
Rabbit
Scotch Beef
Turkey
Venison

CONTENTS

All recipes make four servings

NOTE

For the purposes of this book,
25 grams (g) = 1 ounce (oz),
500 millilitres (ml) = 1 pint (pt).
5 millilitres = one teaspoon (tsp)
10 millilitres = one dessertspoon (dstsp)
15 millilitres = one tablespoon (tbs)

Acknowledgments:
The author and publishers wish to acknowledge the help of the
Emgas Home Advisory Service in the preparation of this book.
Messrs J W Wale and Company of Leicester supplied all the china
used in the photographs.

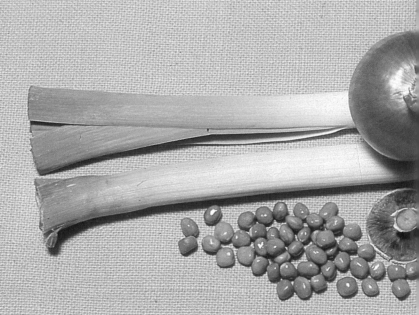

Hot Spicy Pork

Ingredients

4 pork steaks or chops

Marinade

30 ml (2 tbs) oil
1 clove garlic
15-30 ml (1-2 tbs) chilli sauce
30 ml (2 tbs) soy sauce
15 ml (1 tbs) wine vinegar
15 ml (1 tbs) soft brown sugar
15 ml (1 tbs) tomato purée
5 ml (1 tsp) ginger
15 ml (1 tbs) Worcester sauce
Salt and pepper to taste

Method

1 Mix all the ingredients for the marinade.

2 Marinate the pork overnight.

3 Grill the steaks, coat well with marinade whilst grilling.

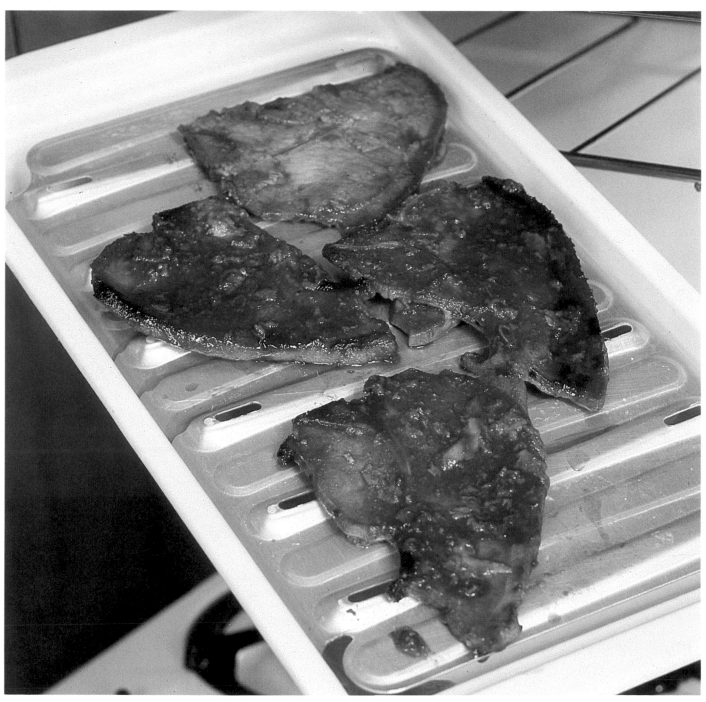

Banana Crunchy Pie

Ingredients

75 g (3 oz) margarine
30 ml (2 level tbs) cocoa
6 level tbs golden syrup
75 g (3 oz) cornflakes

Filling

30 ml (2 level tbs) custard powder
15 ml (1 tbs) granulated sugar
250 ml (½ pt) milk
Dessert topping mix

2 bananas
Grated chocolate or chocolate flake

Method

1 Lightly grease a 20 cm (8 in) flan ring or dish.

2 Put the margarine, cocoa and golden syrup in a pan and heat gently.

3 Crush the cornflakes and, when the margarine has melted, add them to the pan.

4 Mix thoroughly, and press into the base of the dish; leave to set.

5 Place custard powder and sugar in a pan, blend in 250 ml (½ pt) of milk, bring to the boil and cook for a few minutes, stirring all the time.

6 Leave to cool – cover the surface with greaseproof paper to prevent a skin forming.

7 Make up the dessert topping, as directed on the packet.

8 Reserve some of the topping for decoration and whisk the remainder into the cooled custard.

9 Slice the bananas, place in the base of dish. Cover with the custard mixture.

10 Decorate with the reserved topping and grated chocolate or pieces of chocolate flake and sliced banana.

Quick Chilli con Carne

Ingredients

3 onions
100g (4 oz) streaky bacon
2 cloves garlic
22½ ml (1½ tbs) cooking oil
400g (1 lb) minced beef
200g (8 oz) tin baked beans
25g (1 oz) sultanas

1 bay leaf
10 ml (1 dstsp) Demerara sugar
½ level tsp (good pinch) chilli powder
15 ml (1 tbs) tomato purée
125 ml (¼ pt) beef stock
200g (8 oz) patna rice

Method

1 Peel and chop the onions, finely.

2 Remove the bacon rind and chop bacon into small pieces.

3 Crush or chop the garlic.

4 Heat the oil and fry the onions until soft, add the bacon. When both are starting to brown, lift them onto a plate, with a draining spoon.

5 Add the mince to the pan and fry quickly for a few minutes.

6 Turn the meat, bacon, onion and garlic into a saucepan.

7 Add the baked beans, sultanas, bay leaf, sugar, chilli powder, tomato purée and stock.

8 Cover the pan, and bring to the boil. Reduce the heat and cook gently for 45 minutes. Remove bay leaf before serving.

9 Meanwhile, cook the rice in boiling salted water for about 12 minutes. Drain well.

6

Apricot Bordelaise

Ingredients

150g (6 oz) shortcrust pastry
2 egg yolks
50g (2 oz) caster sugar
25g (1 oz) plain flour
250 ml (½ pt) milk
Almond essence, to taste
25g (1 oz) butter
Tall can of apricot halves
25g (1 oz) flaked almonds
50g (2 oz) icing sugar

Method

1 Line a 20 cm (8 in) flan ring with the shortcrust pastry. Bake 'blind' (see page 22) at Gas Mark 6 (400°F/200°C) for 15-20 minutes.

2 Whisk the egg yolks and sugar together until it becomes thick and lighter in colour. Whisk in the flour.

3 Heat the milk, but do not boil.

4 Pour the hot milk over the egg mixture, whisking all the time.

5 Rinse the milk pan with cold water, return the sauce to the pan and bring to the boil, stirring all the time.

6 Flavour with a few drops of almond essence and stir in the butter.

7 Drain the apricots and arrange the fruit in the bottom of the pastry case.

8 Spread the sauce on top of the apricots and cover thickly with sieved icing sugar; top with nuts.

9 Brown under a hot grill.

Plaited Cheese Slice

Ingredients

2 medium sized tomatoes
100g (4 oz) mushrooms
25g (1 oz) margarine
Large packet puff pastry

200g (8 oz) cheese, grated
Salt and pepper to taste
Egg, to glaze

Method

1 Skin and slice tomatoes. Wash and slice the mushrooms.

2 Melt the margarine in a small pan, add the mushrooms, fry for about a minute, drain.

3 Roll out the pastry and trim to an oblong, 30 cm × 23 cm (12 in × 9 in).

4 Mix the grated cheese, tomatoes, mushrooms and seasoning.

5 Spread the mixture down the centre of the pastry, leaving about 2.5 cm (1 in) at each side.

6 Make diagonal cuts at 1.25 cm (½ in) intervals along both sides of the pastry. Brush the pastry with the egg glaze.

7 Bring up strips of pastry from each side alternately to form a plait.

8 Place on a damp baking sheet and brush again with the egg glaze.

9 Bake at Gas Mark 7 (425°F/220°C) for 25-30 minutes.

Rhubarb Fool

Ingredients

400g (1 lb) rhubarb
Sugar to taste
60 ml (4 tbsp) water
Rind of ½ lemon
Juice of 1 lemon
125 ml (¼ pt) double cream
125 ml (¼ pt) milk
10 ml (1 dstsp) custard powder
10 ml (1 dstsp) sugar

Method

1 Cut the rhubarb into small pieces, and stew with the lemon rind and juice and water until tender.

2 Rub through a sieve to make a purée.

3 Make the custard and cool.

4 Half-whip cream, i.e. until it just leaves a trail.

5 Add the custard to the purée, sweeten to taste.

6 Fold in the cream and pour the fool into the serving dishes.

7 Leave to set in the refrigerator.

Variations

Any soft fruit may be used, e.g. gooseberries.

Haddock Deane

Ingredients

400g (1 lb) haddock
200g (8 oz) tomatoes,
  skinned and sliced
12½g (½ oz) butter
50g (2 oz) button mushrooms, sliced
12½g (½ oz) flour
125 ml (¼ pt) dry cider
15 ml (1 level tbs) chopped parsley
Salt and pepper to taste

Topping

75g (3 oz) ground hazelnuts
75g (3 oz) grated cheese
30 ml (2 tbs) milk
30 ml (2 tbs) dry cider
25g (1 oz) butter
50g (2 oz) fresh white breadcrumbs
Pinch of nutmeg
Salt and pepper to taste

Garnish

Lemon twists
Parsley

Method

1 Skin haddock and cut into 2½ cm (1 in) cubes and place in a medium-sized oven-proof dish.

2 Arrange tomato slices on top of fish.

3 Melt butter in a saucepan and fry mushrooms until tender.

4 Stir in the flour and cook for a minute.

5 Remove from heat and stir in the cider, return to the heat and bring to the boil, stirring all the time. Cook for a minute.

6 Add parsley and seasoning.

7 Pour sauce over the fish and tomatoes.

8 Cover and bake at Gas Mark 5 (375°F/190°C) for 20-25 minutes, or until the fish is tender.

9 Mix together the hazelnuts, cheese, milk and cider, and spread on top of fish.

10 Melt butter, add breadcrumbs, nutmeg and seasoning, and sprinkle on top. Dot with butter.

11 Brown under a hot grill.

12 Garnish with lemon twists and parsley.

Orange Tangoes

Ingredients

4 oranges
Ice cream
1 egg
50g (2 oz) caster sugar

Method

1 Cut off the top of the oranges and scoop out the flesh. Chop up into manageable pieces.

2 Pile flesh back into the shells and put a small amount of ice cream on top. Make sure that it is all inside the shell.

3 Separate the egg, whisk the egg white until stiff, add half the sugar and whisk again. When stiff, fold in the remaining sugar.

4 Top oranges with meringue, making sure that all the edges are covered.

5 Cook quickly under a hot grill.

6 Serve at once.

Easter Lamb

Ingredients

800g (2 lb) leg of lamb
1½ lemons
15 ml (1 tbs) oil
Salt and pepper to taste
100g (4 oz) mushrooms
Good pinch of thyme
1 onion
2 sticks of celery
25g (1 oz) butter
125 ml (¼ pt) single cream

Method

1 Cut the lamb into cubes, discard any fat.

2 Place in a bowl. Add the juice of 1 lemon, cut the other half lemon into 4.

3 Add the oil and seasoning to the lamb.

4 Wash and quarter the mushrooms and add with the thyme to the lamb.

5 Cover the meat and marinate for at least 1 hour.

6 Slice onions and thinly slice celery.

7 Melt the butter in a large frying pan, add onions and celery and cook for 10 minutes.

8 Add meat and marinade and cook for 15 minutes, stirring occasionally.

9 Add more seasoning, if necessary.

10 Pour in the cream, but remember not to overheat at this stage.

11 Garnish with lemon quarters.

Hazelnut Cheesecake

Base

50 g (2 oz) margarine
100 g (4 oz) digestive biscuits, crushed
12½ g (½ oz) soft brown sugar

Filling

75 g (3 oz) cream cheese
50 g (2 oz) caster sugar
125 ml (¼ pt) hazelnut yogurt
125 ml (¼ pt) double cream
Blanched hazelnuts
Chocolate flake
Extra cream for decoration

Method

1 Melt the margarine, stir in the biscuit crumbs and sugar. Press into an 18 cm (7 in) flan dish. Chill until firm.

2 Cream the cream cheese and sugar together, stir in the yogurt.

3 Whip the cream until thick, but not until it stands in peaks. Fold the cream into the mixture.

4 Spoon over the base and chill until set.

5 Whip extra cream, about 30-45 ml (2-3 tbs), and pipe rosettes around the top of the cheesecake. Decorate with hazelnuts and crumbled chocolate flake.

Italian Liver

Ingredients

300 g (¾ lb) lamb's liver
250 ml (½ pt) milk
25 g (1 oz) flour
Salt and pepper
37½ g (1½ oz) butter
400 g (1 lb) onions

125 ml (¼ pt) chicken stock
30 ml (2 tbs) tomato purée
1 clove garlic
Good pinch mixed herbs
30 ml (2 tbs) single cream
Parsley, chopped

Method

1 Cut the liver into 2.5 cm (1 in) pieces and soak in milk for 1 hour.

2 Remove the liver and coat in seasoned flour. Melt the butter in a frying pan, fry the liver until brown, remove from the pan.

3 Fry the onions slowly, until tender. Gradually stir in the stock, milk, tomato purée, herbs and garlic. Bring to the boil, stirring all the time.

4 Add the liver to the sauce.

5 Cover the pan and cook gently for 10-15 minutes until the liver is tender. Adjust the seasoning.

6 Place liver and sauce in a serving dish. Trickle cream over the liver and sprinkle with chopped parsley.

7 Serve with creamed potatoes and a green vegetable.

Soufflé Omelette

Ingredients

3 eggs
15 ml (1 tbs) caster sugar
15 ml (1 tbs) milk
Knob of butter
Jam
Icing sugar

Method

1 Separate the eggs. Whisk the egg yolks, sugar and milk until they thicken.

2 Whisk the egg whites, in a clean bowl, until they are stiff and stand in peaks.

3 Fold the egg whites into the egg yolk mixture.

4 Melt the butter in an omelette pan, pour in the egg mixture and cook gently until the base is set and golden brown.

5 Cook top surface under a hot grill, until golden brown, about 2 minutes.

6 Spread jam over half the omelette, fold in half, dredge with icing sugar and serve at once.

15

Summer Recipes

Starters
Tomato Juice Cocktail

Ingredients

500 ml (1 pt) tomato juice
Rind of ½ lemon, grated
Juice of ½ lemon
5 ml (1 tsp) Worcester sauce
Sugar, salt and pepper to taste
Grated nutmeg

Method

1 Combine all the ingredients together.

2 Pour into a jug and chill before serving.

Smoked Mackerel Pâté

Ingredients

200g (8 oz) smoked mackerel, boned and skinned
50g (2 oz) butter, softened
10 ml (1 dstsp) horseradish sauce
10 ml (1 dstsp) lemon juice
Fresh ground pepper

Method

1 Mix all ingredients together, adding pepper to taste.

2 Put in a dish, garnish with lemon and parsley.

Kebabs with Barbecue Sauce

Ingredients

8 small onions
8 bacon rolls
4 sausages
200 g (8 oz) pork, cubed
8 button mushrooms
Oil

Method

1 Peel the onions and cook in boiling water for 5 minutes. Form the bacon into rolls. Twist each sausage to make two.

2 Thread the meats and vegetables onto skewers, brush with oil and place under a high grill.

3 Seal the meat, then lower the grill and cook the kebabs through.

4 Serve with barbecue sauce and either patna rice or creamed potatoes.

Barbecue Sauce

25 g (1 oz) butter
2 onions, finely chopped
30 ml (2 tbs) soft brown sugar
30 ml (2 tbs) Worcester sauce
30 ml (2 tbs) vinegar
125 ml (¼ pt) tomato ketchup
125 ml (¼ pt) pineapple juice
Tall can pineapple pieces
60 ml (4 tbs) lemon juice
5 ml (1 tsp) cornflour

Method

1 Melt the butter and fry the onion until tender.

2 Stir in the remaining ingredients, cover and simmer for 15 minutes.

3 Blend a little cold liquid with the cornflour. Add to the sauce and cook until the sauce clears.

4 Serve with the kebabs.

Variations

Try steak, lamb, pineapple cubes, liver, kidney, green or red peppers to ring the changes.

Strawberry Cake

Ingredients

100g (4 oz) margarine
100g (4 oz) sugar
2 eggs

100g (4 oz) self raising flour
A little milk to mix
400g (1 lb) strawberries, hulled

250 ml (½ pt) double cream
Icing sugar

Method

1 Cream the margarine and sugar together until the mixture becomes light and creamy.

2 Beat the eggs and gradually beat into the mixture.

3 Fold in the sieved flour, using a metal spoon.

4 Add a little milk if necessary, to obtain a soft dropping consistency.

5 Line two 18 cm (7 in) sponge tins with greaseproof paper.

6 Divide the mixture between the tins.

7 Cook at Gas Mark 4 (350°F/ 180°C) for 25-35 minutes or until cakes are risen, golden and slightly shrunk from the side of the tins.

8 Turn out onto a cooling rack and cool.

9 Whip the cream, sweeten to taste.

10 Slice two-thirds of strawberries and mix with cream.

11 Spread filling on one sponge, place second sponge on top.

12 Pipe the top with cream, decorate with whole strawberries, and dust with icing sugar.

Bacon and Egg Flan with Salad

Shortcrust Pastry

150g (6 oz) plain flour
Pinch of salt
37½g (1½ oz) margarine
37½g (1½ oz) lard
Water

Filling

12½g (½ oz) margarine
1 onion, chopped
2 rashers of bacon, chopped
50g (2 oz) mushrooms, chopped
2 eggs
125 ml (¼ pt) milk
50g (2 oz) grated cheese

Method

1 Make the pastry by rubbing in the fats into the flour, until the mixture resembles fine breadcrumbs.

2 Add water, about 6 teaspoons, to form a dough. Knead lightly.

3 Roll out and line a 20 cm (8 in) flan ring. Bake 'blind', (using greaseproof paper and beans, or a foil collar) at Gas Mark 7 (425°F/220°C) for 10 minutes.

4 Fry the onion, bacon and mushrooms in the margarine until cooked and lightly browned.

5 Beat the eggs, add the milk and season to taste.

6 Place cooked onion, bacon and mushrooms in the cooked flan case.

7 Pour the egg mixture over.

8 Sprinkle the grated cheese on top and bake at Gas Mark 6 (400°F/200°C) for 25-30 minutes.

9 Garnish with parsley. Serve hot or cold with a side salad and pickle if liked.

Variations

Ham and sweetcorn.
Cheese and leek.

Chocolate and Orange Mousse

Ingredients

75 g (3 oz) chocolate
3 eggs (separated)
12 g (½ oz) butter
Juice and grated rind
*   of half an orange*

To decorate

125 ml (¼ pt) double cream
Chopped nuts

Method

1 Melt chocolate in a bowl over a pan of hot water.

2 Remove chocolate from heat and beat in egg yolks, butter, orange juice and rind.

3 Whisk egg whites until stiff. Fold into chocolate mixture. Spoon into individual serving dishes and leave to set in refrigerator for half an hour.

4 Decorate with chopped nuts and piped whipped cream.

Sausage Pizza

Scone base

200g (8 oz) plain flour
50g (2 oz) margarine
105 ml (7 tbs) milk, approximately

Topping

2 medium onions
12½g (½ oz) margarine
½ level tsp mixed herbs
Salt and pepper to taste
100g (4 oz) Cheddar cheese, grated
200g (8 oz) sausages

Garnish

1 tomato
Parsley

Method

1 Make the dough by rubbing in the margarine and flour.

2 Add milk, to form a soft, but not sticky, dough.

3 Knead lightly.

4 Roll out to a 23 cm (9 in) circle, place on a baking sheet.

5 Peel and chop the onions, fry in the 12½g (½ oz) margarine with the herbs, until the onions are soft. Season.

6 Spread the onion mixture onto the base of the pizza.

7 Sprinkle with grated cheese.

8 Arrange sausages on top, to form a cartwheel.

9 Bake at Gas Mark 6 (400°F/200°C) for 30-35 minutes, or until the scone base is golden brown.

10 Skin the tomato, cut into wedges and place between the sausages. Garnish with parsley.

11 Serve hot or cold, with vegetables or a green salad.

Variations

1 Cheese, onion and tomato.

2 Mushroom, onion, tomato and cheese.

3 Prawn.

4 Sardine.

Honey Lemon Whip

Ingredients

1 carton (125 ml or 5 fl. oz) natural
  yogurt
30 ml (2 tbs) honey
Rind and juice of ½ lemon
1 egg white

Method

1 In a bowl, mix the yogurt, honey
   and lemon juice.

2 Whisk the egg white until stiff,
   fold into the yogurt mixture.

3 Spoon into individual glasses and
   decorate with grated lemon rind
   and a washed leaf.

Bacon Chops with Tomatoes and Mushrooms

Ingredients

4 bacon chops, rind removed
4 tomatoes, halved
200g (8 oz) mushrooms
Oil

Method

1 Remove the grill rack from the pan and place the halves of tomatoes and the washed mushrooms on the base of the pan. Brush with oil.

2 Place the bacon chops on the grill rack and put on top of the vegetables.

3 Grill, turning the chops until cooked.

4 Serve with creamed potatoes, and garnish with the tomatoes and mushrooms.

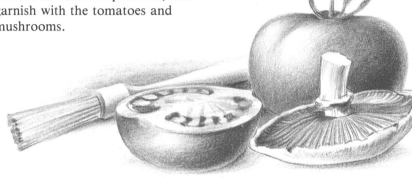

26

Strawberries Cordon Bleu

Ingredients

400 g (1 lb) strawberries
1 orange
30 ml (2 tbs) caster sugar
125 ml (¼ pt) double cream

Method

1 Hull the strawberries and place in a serving dish.

2 Grate rind of orange and place in a bowl with the juice of orange and sugar. Mix well.

3 Lightly whip the cream, fold into the orange mixture. Spoon over the strawberries. Extra cream and fruit can be used to decorate.

4 Chill for 30 minutes before serving.

Variations

Raspberries.
Loganberries.

Autumn Recipes

Lemon-topped Cod
Fruit Jalousie

•

Hamburgers with Sauce
Chilled Lemon Flan

•

Chicken with Pineapple
Steamed Jam Pudding

•

Beef Pot with Horseradish Dumplings
Bramble Sour

•

Sweet and Sour Sausages
Hot Apple Trifle

•

Moussaka
Pear Charlotte

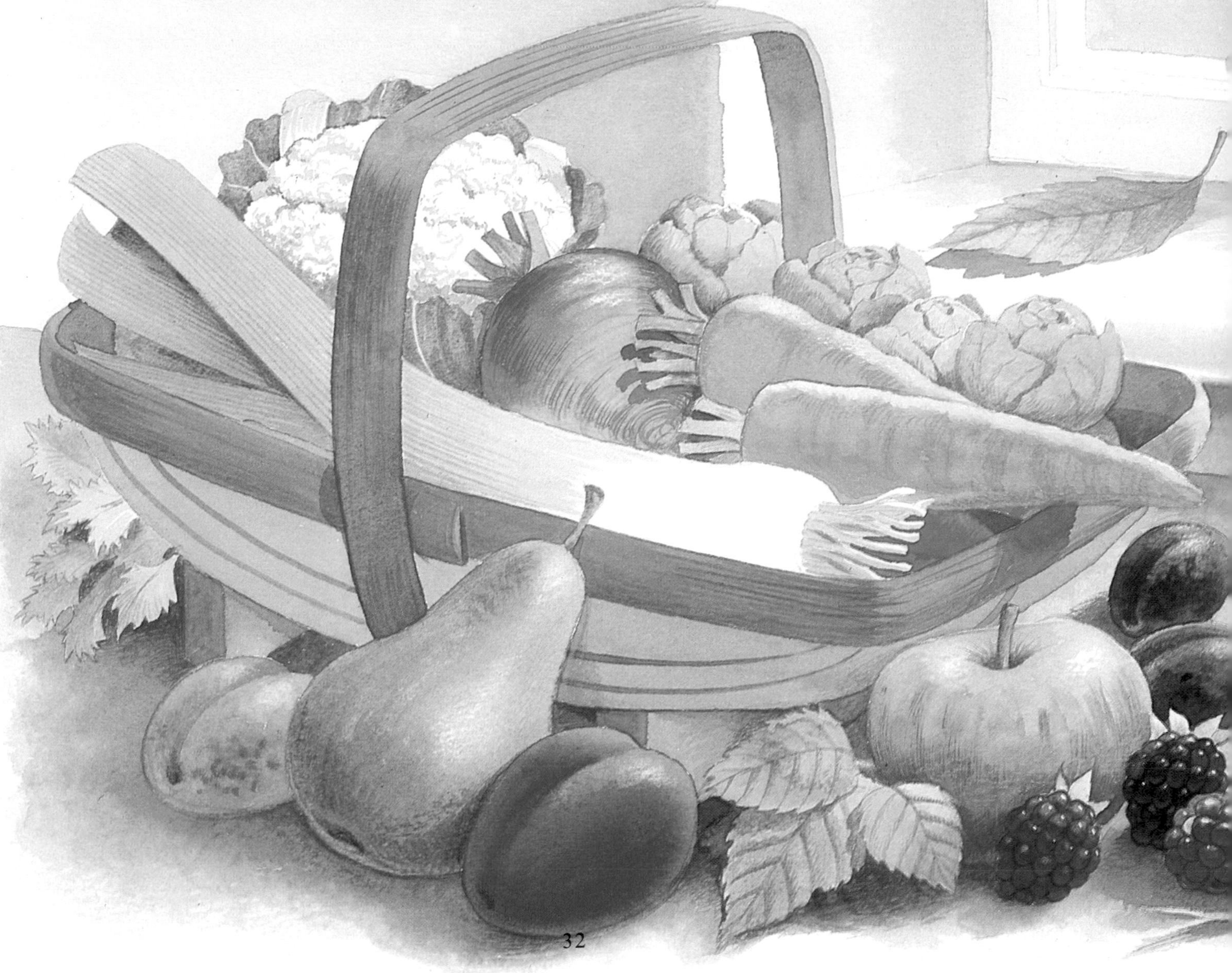

Lemon-topped Cod

Ingredients

4 cod steaks
3 tomatoes, skinned and sliced
100g (4 oz) fresh breadcrumbs
30 ml (2 tbs) fresh parsley, chopped
Grated rind and juice of 1 lemon
Salt and pepper to taste
1 beaten egg
30 ml (2 tbs) water
Oil

Method

1 Place the fish on the grill pan grid.

2 To make the topping, mix all the other ingredients, except the tomatoes.

3 Divide the topping between the steaks.

4 Grill under a medium heat for 15-20 minutes.

5 Place tomato slices on top, brush with oil and grill for a further 5 minutes.

Fruit Jalousie

Ingredients

Small packet frozen puff pastry
Small tin sliced peaches
30-45 ml (2-3 tbs) brown sugar

Method

1 Roll out the pastry to an oblong, 1.5 mm (¹⁄₁₆ in) thickness.

2 Cut the pastry in half and place one half on a dampened baking sheet.

3 Drain the peaches and place down the centre of the pastry.

4 Sprinkle with brown sugar.

5 Fold the second piece of pastry in half lengthwise, and make cuts in the folded edge at 1.25 cm (½ in) intervals. Do not cut to the other edge – leave a border of 2.5 cm (1 in).

6 Brush edges of pastry with water either side of peaches.

7 Place the second piece of pastry on one half of the base, unfold and seal the two together. To make an effective seal, 'knock' the edges together with the back of a knife.

8 Bake at Gas Mark 6 (400°F/200°C) for 25-30 minutes until well risen and golden brown.

Variations

Apricots, cherries or any fruit desired.

Hamburgers with Sauce

Ingredients

400g (1 lb) minced beef
2 onions, chopped
Pinch of garlic salt
Salt and pepper to taste
10 ml (1 dstsp) made mustard
10 ml (1 dstsp) tomato purée
2 eggs beaten
30 ml (2 tbs) chopped parsley

Method

1 Mix all the ingredients together.

2 If you want 'real American' burgers, shape into 2 burgers. If not, shape into 4 burgers.

3 Fry the burgers over a low heat. Allow 8 minutes per side for the large ones.

4 Serve in buttered baps with a salad.

CHOOSE A SAUCE

Southern Style Sauce

Tall tin tomatoes
1 small green pepper, finely chopped
1 onion, sliced
5 ml (1 tsp) sugar
5 ml (1 tsp) dried oregano
Seasoning to taste

Method

1 Put all the ingredients into a pan.

2 Simmer gently for 10-12 minutes.

3 Adjust the seasoning.

Mushroom Sauce

50g (2 oz) mushrooms, chopped
12½ g (½ oz) butter
2 rashers bacon, chopped
½ tin condensed mushroom soup
Seasoning to taste

Method

1 Fry the chopped mushrooms and bacon in the butter until soft.

2 Add the soup and season to taste.

Chilled Lemon Flan

Base

100 g (4 oz) digestive biscuits (broken)
50 g (2 oz) margarine
15 ml (1 level tbs) caster sugar

Filling

125 ml (¼ pt) double cream
150 g (6 oz) condensed milk
2 lemons, rind and juice
Crystallised lemon slices
Whipped cream to decorate

Method

1 Crush the biscuits by placing them in a large polythene bag and hitting them with a rolling pin.

2 Melt the margarine in a pan, add sugar and then blend in the biscuit crumbs. Mix well.

3 Turn mixture into an 18 cm (7 in) flan dish and press firmly into shape round the base and sides.

4 Bake in an oven at Gas Mark 2 (300°F/150°C) for 8 minutes. Remove from the oven and leave to cool.

5 In a large bowl, mix together the cream, condensed milk and finely grated lemon rind.

6 Beat in the lemon juice.

7 Pour mixture into flan case and chill until firm, in the refrigerator.

8 Just before serving, decorate with slices of crystallised lemon and whirls of cream.

Chicken with Pineapple

Ingredients

15 ml (1 tbs) oil
50g (2 oz) blanched almonds
1 small onion, finely sliced
18g (¾ oz) cornflour
500 ml (1 pt) chicken stock

Tall can pineapple rings
200g (8 oz) cooked chicken, cut into
  pieces
200g (8 oz) patna rice
Pimento for garnish

Method

1 Heat the oil and lightly brown the almonds.

2 Remove almonds from the pan.

3 Fry the onion in the remaining oil, until soft and tender.

4 Blend the cornflour with a little of the cold stock, add the remaining stock.

5 Add to the pan and bring to the boil, stirring all the time.

6 Chop half the pineapple into small pieces and add to pan. Add chicken pieces and also browned almonds.

7 Cook for about 3 minutes.

8 Serve on a bed of patna rice.

9 Garnish the chicken with strips of pimento and pineapple.

Steamed Jam Pudding

Ingredients

100 g (4 oz) margarine
100 g (4 oz) caster sugar
150 g (6 oz) self raising flour
Good pinch of salt
Rind of 1 lemon, grated
2 eggs
45 ml (3 tbs) strawberry jam

Method

1 Place all ingredients, except the jam, in a bowl, and beat well.

2 Put the jam at the base of a 750 ml (1½ pt) oven-proof basin.

3 Place pudding mixture in basin on top of jam.

4 Place greaseproof paper and foil on the top and secure.

5 Steam for 1 hour.

6 Turn out and serve with custard.

Variations

Raspberry jam, treacle and golden syrup.

Beef Pot with Horseradish Dumplings

Ingredients

600g (1½ lb) chuck steak
25g (1 oz) plain flour (seasoned)
25g (1 oz) dripping
2 onions, finely sliced
30 ml (2 tbs) tomato purée
Good pinch mixed herbs
2 celery sticks
500 ml (1 pt) beef stock

Dumplings

100g (4 oz) self raising flour
37½ g (1½ oz) shredded suet
5 ml (1 tsp) salt
30 ml (2 tbs) horseradish sauce
30-45 ml (2-3 tbs) water

Method

1 Cut the meat into pieces and toss in the well-seasoned flour.

2 Melt the dripping in a frying pan, add the onion, cook until soft. Add the meat and fry until well browned.

3 Remove from the heat and gradually add the stock, tomato purée, celery and herbs.

4 Return to the heat and bring to the boil.

5 Transfer to a 1½ litre (3 pt) casserole dish. Cover and cook for 2 hours at Gas Mark 4 (350°F/180°C).

6 To make the dumplings, sift together the flour and salt, add the suet. Blend the horseradish sauce and water together. Add to the flour and mix to a soft dough.

7 Shape into 8 small balls, add to the casserole for the last 45 minutes of the cooking time.

Bramble Sour

Ingredients

400g (1 lb) blackberries
75g (3 oz) caster sugar
45 ml (3 tbs) water
5 ml (1 tsp) arrowroot
1 carton soured cream
50-75g (2-3 oz) Demerara sugar

Method

1 Stew the blackberries with sugar and water until soft. Leave to cool.

2 Drain off the liquid and reserve it.

3 Place fruit in a 750 ml (1½ pt) oven-proof dish or individual ramekin dishes.

4 Thicken the liquid by making a smooth paste with a little of the cold blackberry juice and the arrowroot.

5 Place the paste and the rest of the blackberry liquid in a small saucepan. Bring to the boil, stirring all the time, until the sauce clears.

6 Add sauce to blackberries, cover with soured cream.

7 Cover with Demerara sugar and place under a hot grill until the sugar melts and caramelises.

8 Serve at once.

Sweet and Sour Sausages

Ingredients

8 skinless sausages
30 ml (2 tbs) oil
1 onion, sliced
1 green pepper, deseeded and sliced
1 small can pineapple slices
15 ml (1 tbs) cornflour
1 chicken stock cube
5 ml (1 tsp) Worcester sauce
15 ml (1 tbs) sweet chutney
1 large tomato, skinned
200 g (8 oz) patna rice

Method

1 Cut the sausages into 5 cm (2 in) pieces, heat the oil in a frying pan and brown the sausages.

2 Add the onion and pepper and fry for 2 minutes.

3 Drain pineapple, cut into quarters. Save the juice, make it up to 250 ml (½ pt) with water.

4 Blend cornflour with a little of the juice to a smooth paste, add rest of the juice.

5 Add to the pan, crumble in the stock cube, add the Worcester sauce and chutney. Cut pineapple and tomato into pieces and add. Stir well.

6 Cook slowly over a low heat for 10 minutes, stirring occasionally.

7 Meanwhile, cook the rice in a saucepan of boiling salted water.

8 Serve sausages on a bed of rice.

Hot Apple Trifle

Ingredients

4 trifle sponges
200g (8 oz) apple slices
Lemon juice
Water

500 ml (1 pt) thick custard
2 egg whites
75g (3 oz) caster sugar
Flaked almonds
Glacé cherries

As an extra special touch, soak the trifle sponges in a small amount of sherry.

Method

1 Gently poach the apple slices in a little lemon juice and water. Cool.

2 Cut trifle sponges in half and arrange on the base of a 750 ml (1½ pt) oven-proof dish.

3 Cover with apples and then pour the custard over.

4 Whisk the egg-whites until stiff, gradually whisk in the sugar. Pipe or spread over the custard.

5 Decorate with the almonds and cherries.

6 Bake at Gas Mark 3 (325°F/160°C) for 20-25 minutes.

7 Serve at once.

Moussaka

Ingredients

1 can minced steak (400g or 1 lb)
1 large onion, peeled and sliced
25g (1 oz) lard
15-30 ml (1-2 tbs) tomato purée
Small tin new potatoes

25g (1 oz) margarine
25g (1 oz) flour
250 ml (½ pt) milk
Salt and pepper to taste
100g (4 oz) grated cheese

Method

1 Place the steak in an oven-proof dish.

2 Melt the lard and fry the sliced onions until soft.

3 Add the onion and tomato purée to the dish, mix in.

4 Drain and slice the potatoes, arrange over the meat.

5 Make the sauce by putting the margarine, flour and milk into a saucepan. Bring to the boil, whisking all the time. Cook for a few minutes after the sauce has boiled.

6 Stir in half the cheese, season to taste, pour over the potatoes.

7 Sprinkle with remaining cheese and bake at Gas Mark 5 (375°F/190°C) for about 30 minutes.

8 Serve with green peas or beans.

Pear Charlotte

Ingredients

400g (1 lb) pears
75 ml (5 tbs) brown sugar
60 ml (4 tbs) apricot jam
6 slices white bread
100g (4 oz) melted butter

Method

1 Peel, core and slice pears, put half in a well-buttered 1 litre (2 pt) oven-proof dish.

2 Sprinkle 30 ml (2 tbs) sugar over the pears and spread with 30 ml (2 tbs) jam.

3 Cover with remaining pears, 30 ml (2 tbs) sugar, and jam.

4 Remove crusts from the bread, cut each slice into 4 triangles. Dip into melted butter and arrange on top of the pears, covering them completely.

5 Sprinkle with remaining sugar.

6 Bake at Gas Mark 6 (400°F/200°C) for 30 minutes until crisp and golden.

7 Serve hot with cream.

Winter Recipes

French Onion Soup
Pork Chops
with Apple and Raisin Sauce
Banana Crescents

•

Easy Vegetable Soup
Turkey and Ham Risotto
Cheese and Biscuits

•

Mince Soufflé
Mandarin and Grape Flan

•

Macaroni Italienne
Chocolate Pie

•

Turkey Provençale
Mincemeat and Peach Crumble

French Onion Soup

Ingredients

300 g (12 oz) onions
30 ml (2 tbs) oil
1½ litres (3 pts) beef stock
6 thin slices of French bread
150 g (6 oz) grated cheese

Method

1 Peel the onions and slice thinly.

2 Heat the fat in a large frying pan or saucepan. Fry the onions, gently, until golden brown.

3 Stir in the stock and cook for approximately 10 minutes.

4 Toast the French bread.

5 Pour the soup into 6 individual oven-proof soup bowls or 1 large oven-proof soup bowl.

6 Sprinkle the cheese over the toast and float the toast on the soup.

7 Place under the grill for about 5 minutes, and serve immediately.

Variations

The soup may be made richer by the addition of an egg yolk, or port may be added just before serving.

Pork Chops with Apple and Raisin Sauce

Ingredients

4 pork chops
25 g (1 oz) margarine
½ green pepper,
    deseeded and chopped
250 ml (½ pt) chicken stock
50 g (2 oz) raisins
2 cooking apples, peeled, cored and
    sliced
5 ml (1 tsp) lemon rind, grated
1 bay leaf
Salt and pepper to taste
15-30 ml (1-2 tbs) tomato purée

Method

1 Grill the pork chops, allowing 10 minutes each side.

2 Meanwhile prepare the sauce: melt the margarine in a saucepan, add the green pepper and fry for about 5 minutes or until soft.

3 Add all the remaining ingredients and simmer the sauce for 10 minutes or until the apple is cooked.

4 Remove the bay leaf and pour sauce over the chops.

5 Decorate with slices of green pepper.

Banana Crescents

Ingredients

1 large packet puff pastry
15 ml (1 tbs) caster sugar
1 level tsp cinnamon

4 bananas
Beaten egg
Icing sugar

Method

1 Roll out the pastry into a 30 cm (12 in) circle.

2 Cut into quarters, and then into eight.

3 Mix the caster sugar and cinnamon together and sprinkle over the pastry.

4 Peel the bananas and cut in half.

5 Place half a banana on each piece of pastry and roll up.

6 Brush each tip of pastry with a little beaten egg and press down.

7 Place on a dampened baking sheet with the tip underneath.

8 Brush with beaten egg and bake at Gas Mark 7 (425°F/220°C) for 15-20 minutes.

9 When cool, dust with icing sugar.

Easy Vegetable Soup

Ingredients

500 ml (1 pt) water
1 litre (2 pts) chicken stock
1 small packet frozen mixed vegetables
2 sticks celery, finely chopped
25 g.(1 oz) plain flour
25 g (1 oz) butter or margarine
Dash of Worcester sauce
Salt and pepper to taste
Chopped parsley

Method

1 Place all ingredients, except the parsley, in a medium-sized saucepan; bring to the boil.

2 Simmer gently for about 10 minutes.

3 If a cream soup is required, liquidise at this point.

4 Check the seasoning.

5 Sprinkle with chopped parsley before serving.

Turkey and Ham Risotto

Ingredients

37½ g (1½ oz) lard or margarine
1 onion, sliced
50g (2 oz) mushrooms, sliced
1 green pepper, sliced
200g (8 oz) patna rice
750 ml (1½ pts) stock
Salt and pepper to taste
300g (12 oz) turkey pieces (cooked)
100g (4 oz) ham pieces (cooked)
Grated cheese

Method

1 Melt the fat in a large saucepan, add the sliced onion, mushrooms and pepper. Fry the vegetables gently, until the onion is soft.

2 Add the rice and fry gently for 2 minutes.

3 Add the stock.

4 Cook for 25 minutes.

5 Add the seasoning, chicken and ham and cook for another 5 minutes.

6 Serve with grated cheese.

Variations

Instead of turkey, use chicken.

50

Cheese and Biscuits

Some of the more popular cheeses which are readily available

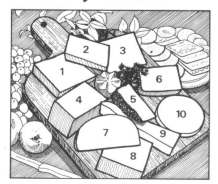

1 **Wensleydale** – a crumbly mild cheese which is traditionally served with apple pie in the North.

2 **Double Gloucester** with chives and onions has a firm smooth texture, and is excellent with crusty bread.

3 **Cheshire** cheese can be white or red, and has a slightly salty, savoury taste. It is the oldest British cheese.

4 **Leicester** is a mild cheese with a flaky texture. A good cooking cheese.

5 **Tome au Raisin** is a white, strong-flavoured cheese from France, covered with a mixture of dried grapeskins and pips.

6 **Danish Blue** (sometimes called Danablu) has a strong salty flavour and a soft, slightly crumbly texture.

7 **Edam** is a mild cheese from Holland with a smooth, slightly rubbery texture.

8 **Sage Derby** is produced by adding chopped fresh sage in layers during the making of this mild, close-textured cheese.

9 **Brie** – even the crust is edible on this delicately flavoured French cheese. At its best from October to June. To find out if Brie is ripe, press the surface and the cheese should bulge but not run.

10 **German smoked cheese** is mild and creamy with a smooth texture.

Mince Soufflé

Ingredients

2 onions
100g (4 oz) mushrooms
400g (1 lb) minced beef
45 ml (3 tbs) oil
Seasoning
3 eggs
Small packet instant potato
25g (1 oz) butter
30 ml (2 tbs) milk
10 ml (1 dstsp) chopped parsley
Large pinch of ground nutmeg

Method

1 Peel the onions and chop finely. Wash and slice the mushrooms.

2 Fry the vegetables and meat in the oil for 5 minutes until brown. Season to taste. Pour into a medium-sized soufflé dish.

3 Separate the eggs.

4 Make up instant potato as directed on the packet. Beat in butter, milk, egg yolks, chopped parsley and nutmeg. Add salt and pepper if necessary.

5 Whisk egg whites until stiff, fold into the potato mixture and put on top of the mince.

6 Bake at Gas Mark 5 (375°F/190°C) for about 45 minutes until cooked and golden brown.

7 Serve immediately.

Mandarin and Grape Flan

Sponge

2 eggs
50g (2 oz) caster sugar
50g (2 oz) plain flour

Filling

Medium-sized tin mandarins
50g (2 oz) green or black grapes
Quick-jel

Method

1 Whisk the eggs and sugar until thick and creamy.

2 Sift the flour and gently fold into the egg mixture, using a metal spoon.

3 Pour into a greased sponge flan tin, bake at Gas Mark 5 (375°F/190°C) for 15-20 minutes. Leave to cool.

4 Drain the mandarins and save some of the juice to make up the Quick-jel.

5 Halve the grapes and remove all the pips.

6 Arrange the fruit in the base of the sponge.

7 Make up the Quick-jel as instructed and pour over the fruit.

A bought sponge flan case saves time.

53

Macaroni Italienne

Ingredients

1 green pepper
200g (8 oz) cooked ham or bacon
4 tomatoes
200g (8 oz) macaroni
1 medium can condensed mushroom
  soup
Salt and pepper to taste
50g (2 oz) grated cheese

This dish can be made in advance and reheated in a moderate oven.

Method

1 Dice the pepper, remove all seeds. Cut and dice the ham or bacon.

2 Cook the macaroni in boiling, salted water for 7 minutes, drain and rinse with hot water.

3 Make up the soup with half a can of water, and bring slowly to the boil, stirring all the time.

4 Remove from the heat, add macaroni, ham, green pepper and seasoning.

5 Turn into a shallow 1 litre (2 pt) oven-proof dish.

6 Sprinkle with cheese.

7 Skin and slice the tomatoes.

8 Arrange a row of tomato slices on top of the macaroni.

9 Grill until golden brown and bubbling.

10 Serve immediately.

Chocolate Pie

Base

200g (8 oz) digestive biscuits
50g (2 oz) butter
30 ml (2 tbs) golden syrup

Filling

1 packet chocolate Instant Whip
250 ml (½ pt) milk
Small tin evaporated milk
Grated chocolate
Flaked almonds

To make sure that evaporated milk will whip easily, simply store in the refrigerator.

Method

1 Crush the biscuits. Melt the butter and syrup in a saucepan. Add the biscuits and mix well.

2 Press into an 18 cm (7 in) flan dish. Chill well.

3 Make up the Instant Whip, as directed.

4 Whip up the evaporated milk and fold it into the Instant Whip.

5 Turn into the biscuit crust.

6 Decorate with grated chocolate and flaked almonds.

Turkey Provençale

Ingredients

4 cooked turkey portions
or 400g (1 lb) cooked turkey pieces
50g (2 oz) margarine
50g (2 oz) flour
1 sliced onion
50g (2 oz) stuffed olives
15 ml (1 level tbs) tomato purée
375 ml (¾ pt) chicken stock
2 oranges
Salt and pepper to taste
Parsley

Method

1 Melt the fat and fry the onions until soft, but not too brown.

2 Add the flour gradually, stir in, add the tomato purée and stock. Bring to the boil, stirring all the time, and cook the sauce for about 3 minutes.

3 Add the turkey, sliced oranges (reserve some for garnish) and olives. Cook for a further 5 minutes, to heat everything through.

4 Season to taste.

5 Serve with tagliatelle and garnish with orange slices and parsley.

56

Mincemeat and Peach Crumble

Ingredients

100g (4 oz) plain flour
50g (2 oz) margarine
50g (2 oz) ground almonds

50g (2 oz) caster sugar
120 ml (8 tbs) mincemeat
Medium-sized tin sliced peaches
Glacé cherries

Method

1 Rub the fat into the flour until the mixture resembles fine breadcrumbs.

2 Add the ground almonds and sugar and mix thoroughly.

3 Place mincemeat at the base of a 500 ml (1 pt) oven-proof dish. Cover with some of the sliced peaches.

4 Top with the crumble mixture.

5 Decorate with the remaining peaches and glacé cherries.

6 Bake at Gas Mark 6 (400°F/200°C) for 45 minutes.

Variations

Apricot slices, sliced apple.